A Breath Before Dying

By

Geoff Francis

Published in Great Britain in 2019 by Bonobo TV
This edition 2019

ISBN   978-1-907729-30-0

Edited by Jacky Francis
Designed by Paul Windridge

www.bonobo.tv

A Breath Before Dying

For Freddie
and all the others

A Breath Before Dying is a long form poem which looks at the experience of having someone you love who has a progressive terminal illness. Setting it in the context of an enduring love affair intensifies the sense of what has been lost. The intangibility of the passion that once was lives as a ghost in only one memory and poignantly intrudes and disrupts the everyday of the survivor. The words and emotions evoked take us into the world of prolonged bereavement without death.

Life expectancy is uncertain. The remainder of our life span is decreasing continually. There'll come a time when all of us must leave here. Good health is simply the slowest way a human being can die. What happens when health fails and dignity is lost? Wealth cannot help us. We can be kept living, but just being alive is not living. The tragedy is that even our loved ones cannot help, no matter how we might plead with them or with anyone who can hear our voice.

All of us will have had heartache in our lives. One of the most heartrending moments of my life was to witness my late father's response to a dementia test. His diagnosis was vascular dementia. But by whatever name it goes, the sudden realisation of the extent of the faculties a loved one has lost tears the heart out of those who are a witness to it day to day. Only those who have gone through this most destructive experience truly understand how It affects their own lives and health.

Loss in life is inevitably hard to take. But loss while the other is still physically present can be the most painful. Until they are gone, until you know the outcome, there is no closure. But wishing an end to their indignity and distress, being helpless to grant their wish to end their life early, does not come without its own pernicious form of grief and guilt.

"Euthanasia is the act or practice of killing, or permitting the death, of hopelessly sick or injured individuals (such as persons or domestic animals) in a relatively painless way for reasons of mercy." https://www.merriam-webster.com/dictionary/euthanasia The word originated in the early 17th century from the Greek eu 'good' and thanatos 'death'.

UK law currently denies a person the right to assistance in ending their own life. A 2015 Populus poll found that 82% of people supported assisted dying, including 86% of people with disabilities. In 2017 a poll on Doctors.net.uk, published in the British Medical Journal, said that 55% of doctors would support assisted dying. Over 41m Commonwealth citizens and 60m American citizens can have choice and control over their death, but Britain's elected representatives fearfully lag behind lawmakers overseas and public opinion at home. 'The law on assisted dying in Britain is incoherent and hypocritical. It makes a mockery of due process, is inhumane, and needs to change,' says Lord Falconer, Britain's Lord Chancellor from 2003 to 2007 and chair of the Commission on Assisted Dying.

A statement made by the European Court of Human Rights in 2002 acknowledged, "In an era of growing medical sophistication, combined with longer life expectancies, many people are concerned that they should not be forced to linger on in old age or in states of advanced physical or mental decrepitude which conflict with strongly held ideas of self and personal identity." Yet 46 Britons a year have no choice but to go to Switzerland for an assisted suicide with Dignitas. The first organisation of this kind in the world, Dignitas was founded in 1998 by a human-rights lawyer.

In order to assist the process for those who cannot find the means to go to Switzerland, a number of compassionate individuals have created 'euthanasia machines', engineered to allow terminally ill people to die by voluntary euthanasia or assisted suicide without prolonged pain. They may be operated by a second person or by the person themselves. Examples include the Thanatron and Mercitron, invented by Jack Kevorkian, plus the Deliverance Machine, The Exit International euthanasia device and the Sarco machine, all created by Philip Nitschke.

There is a wide range of organisations all over the world campaigning for individuals to have the right to control their own departure from this world and for it to be legal to have assistance to do so. Details can be found on the internet, however Dignity in Dying seems to have the highest profile in the UK, with patrons including prominent individuals from the worlds of business, politics, the arts and religion, such as Sir Terry Pratchett, Dr Jonathan Miller, Patricia Hewitt, Zoë Wanamaker, Simon Weston, Patrick Stewart, Anthony Grayling and Matthew Wright.

https://www.dignityindying.org.uk

the old man sits
on Their bench
  his wife beside him
  in Her wheelchair

together
they watch the river's flow
 and feel the water's freshness

 as a gift
in the sunshine

and
the shadows

                                    some time
                                    each day
                                    often in
                            each cheating hour
                                    she is lost
                            drifts further away
                                    from him
                            from all she knew
                                    and wanted

                                    unstoppable
                            like the waters they watch

                                    and all the love
                                    he gives
                                    is not enough

Year upon
Recent year
They had grown
too old
for the weather

For the wind
and rain

but mostly
The wind
that cut
through
them

Chilled
them
to the bone

lassoed
their feet
and dragged
them deep
to a place
where
no lessons
could be found

all that lay there
was a desperate desire
to escape

was it only human beings
who made life's experiment
so painful?
He was feeling like a fraud
Who Can't face truthfully
The daily diminishing of her reality
Watching her Lost in her remaining whatever time

a fraud

Who Can't face
The certainty of the distance between them
To feel her forever gone

a fraud

Who Can't face
That death
which would lose every how
Of seeing her again

finally telling
the truth he had weaved
And held on to
through the years

a fraud

Who can't face
His impossible tasks
And has given up on the trying
To trade them
into an exchange
riddled with complacency

a fraud

Who can't face
The certainty
That they all
will discover
The truth

Some day
Sooner
Or
Later

He stands on a dissolving precipice
Inviting the chaos
Where his final epitaph Will Lie
Appropriately lost
amongst the confusion
Of whatever
he thought he was

When he looked back
With the eyes of today
He knew
There was a time
When he could
Have changed it all

when
He believed
That all you needed
Was love
To infect
Those who resisted

And those who orchestrated
The games
In which imagination's dance
was Loose and free
Cannot be heard clearly

in the passage
of a time now lost
they sit In rooms
Of Half grasped
Memory

Holding tight
Onto
Something
they once truly knew
So far from now

Looking again
At words
Which mean nothing
To her

Names of places
Where they had
Never been

Challenging
Why
they should
Need to exist
As Part
Of her world

Inside her truth
They held
No proximity
No reality
Or distance

Innocently
she set out
An ever widening
Space about her
Where she could survive
Slow

 And
could
Embrace
What was
 in
 the time left

That unassailable wish
Unrealisable
Unfulfillable

He
Wanted her
Needed her
To tell him
What was true

Where the pleasure
Lay
Had Lain

Not
to pretend
Or
Lie
Accepting
His weight
Upon her
Or
him
Inside her
Irrespective
Of her joy
Or delight

And now
He
Could not know

The silenced voice
Could never
Answer

He had come
To desperately need
the way
the day
did not
begin

until

they exchanged
some words

not important

what was said
nothing significant
or world shattering

no obvious
statements of affection

it was
just the presence
of the words
where the warmth lay

looking back
life had been
so empty
just
because
it had been
so full of nothing important

Except

when he had touched
her softness
and every part
of him
grew full
in that caress

and its pleasure
shared

there was nothing more
nothing less

it surprised him still
how they once had lived
so separately
yet become a match
in their isolation

not by compromise
no reaching for the sky
just to surrender

unwilling to brook
less
than each
required of life
unfettered
by any convention

willing to accept love
from each other
alone

a purpose fulfilled

letting him know
just how much
he could be alone
and remain in love

even when
oblivion's call
wrestled her
into its embrace

wanting her
to disperse
and fade
with the true
nothingness of being

witnessing that embrace
every vestige
he had contrived
to dress this lifetime
was stripped from him

each atom
found a part
in eternal stillness

In that embrace
because of her
he was certain

that above the clouds
the Sun
found moments of forever

never a dream
all ways real

he had never found her in dreams

had he known
she was there
the travelling
would have been
so much easier

lighted and lightened
by a freedom
held tight
locked close in a kiss

for ever

outside time
in their own part
of eternity

Replete in love

surrendering to her
surrendering to them

willing

to yield to life
and all it may bring

certain

in the knowing
they had reached
a meaning

loose of
Earth's binding
Daedalus falling
from the blissful touch
of the Sun

the price
of submission to
the delirium
of unexpected love

yet within their touch
 life was wider
 fuller
 more complete

their kiss
 had touched him
 where no one
had ever
been allowed

 into his chest
an exquisite
 incision

 to reveal
a truth

 a reason

Moving through her days slowly
Barely conscious
Perhaps hoping for an end
in some reason to have been

What she thought
she had once known
was of no importance now

to satisfy
some perverse caprice
the Fates
who
had gifted
them love
now thwarted
his life's purpose

he made a promise
into
her uncomprehending ear
that an aged orpheus
would seek them out
bring light in their darkest places
to bring retribution upon their perfidy

Unheard

                                    he told her
                                they should live
                                    she and he
                                    in a place
                            where others understood
                                the value of love

                                        and if
                            they could not find
                                    that place
                            they should make it anew
                            over whatever lifetimes
                                        until
                                they could embrace
                                    in one soul
                                        again

No matter where
He stood
This road
Would remain the same
unchanged
By time
Or distance

Perhaps one day
One lifetime
He would walk
that road again

and see
for the first time
The victims Of his progress

From within his confusion
He Cast out
a hopefilled net
Of compassion
For the meaning
Of their lives
And his own

An everlasting
Blessing
For an eventual understanding
Of how
Or what
Or why

Sometimes often
They would lay
mouth upon mouth

Her kiss
would suck him in
to
a place
where time
has no point
or purpose
No relevance at all

It was theirs
alone
to share

it drew upon the spirit

                                      that moves the Spring

It was obvious
that the time left
was far shorter
than the time past

Memories held
had more import
than any future actions
or thoughts

unless he changed

It was his favourite time
he felt justified
when the end of the day came

                                        she did not
                                        know that
                                   she was the place
                                  to which he would
                                    always return
                                  when so many others
                                     who had tried to
                                     to hold him did

                                     he had cried
                                       and lied
                                      he wanted
                                 to burst like the storm

                        just what reason would end his life

21

what happy moment
turned sour and sad

or would it be
a sad moment made happy in his release

he had given her back
her love

her dreams
unopened
unread

how cruel
was he
when
he
had returned them
once more

Words
None spoken
Disintegrated
In time
Like
Her once sweet body
Laid lifeless
In the ground

Rooms
Empty

Bereft
Of All
But for
Neverwere ghosts

In him
She had tripped
a sensing
of desire

not just his own
but hers too
running deeper
more open

not fired
by temporary longing

rather
something
he could savour
slowly
in every moment she dwelt
in his thoughts

sweet
and special

outside
of their time

life took on
a relaxed urgency
to tell
all
of the little
he
had come

to understand

                              Looking back
                         it was a wonder
                                      how
                          like their bodies
                               two lives
                              had fitted
                             so together
                         had become one

                              Hiroshima
                    shadow marked moments

                          As if her body
                      hung in the branches
                         a leopard's prey
                       above in every tree
                          he passed under

                                  until
                      the vultures recycled it

The two most precious things
in his life
had started
in one place

They belonged
to that place

when they had gone
his heart
had grown sick
there

yet it seemed
it was there
that he had to wait
until it gave up
completely

In these moments
no well rehearsed bravado
could allow him to hide
the tender child's fear
that had been his birthright

In those moments
the choice was made
to care
or not to dare

To reject the fear
and its easy consequence
of greed

and nurture
the legacy
that breath can bring.

or stay
just
where he was
choking on his own excess

an unconscious
daylight sleepwalker
crushing the world
with every step

                    with each easter light
                              she came

                    holding in her hands
                              each dream
                         they had shared

                              telling him
                         of what he could
                              have been

            leaving only a bitter tear
                          in the night

The middle of the night
had long become
a place
to contemplate

where childlike dreams
might roam free

curled close
safe

always there

a reassuring
hand to hold onto

to touch
to hold

then
it had become
a realm
of nightmares

where she wandered a wasteland
deleted of
memory

where he might
become the enemy

Each encounter there
left his flesh bruised
his spirit
depleted and devastated

There dwelt
the now of emptiness

No hand to hold
No warmth to touch

He turned over
in the hope
that sleep
would return
and spare him from
any such pointless
troubled and
troubling thought

Unfulfilled
Lost
In the vision
Made up
From memory
Of long ago

Of a parting
pleading
Smile

And this year
he missed the day
he had missed so long ago

The armour he wore
his protection
against the world
was so fragile
when he stared
into
her hazel eyes
 in dreams

where he sought
his truth
his freedom

far from
the treachery of
every day

They had always been
Ready to surrender
all they had learned
and known

one to the other

before
the consequences
of age
took
and wracked
their being
and robbed
them both
of the opportunity
of understanding
why life

                                              had been
                                             as it had
                                        and allow them
                                             the right
                                              to know
                                                  why

                                    they stood naked then

face to face
seeking
the delightful oblivion
of a kiss
deep enough
to touch
inside each mind
and remove
the pain
that lies there

to take a chance
on love's temporary
tender moments
which do not tie

each one wanting
the other
to stay free
and alone
on the path
they had always trod

Their conversation

so often
was mundane

but never
empty

Never unnecessary

now and then
so deep
so honest
so profound
it caught
him by surprise

with such
a rich pleasure

He had loved it
when
she had said
that
time
was special

he could
admit that truth

and

                                    when
                         in the darkness
                          he came upon
                                moments
                             that froze
                                his soul

                               he knew
                                    she
                     would understand

                                    she
                              wouldn't
                          have to try

                              she just
                                 would

so Many times
She did not
Understand
The Meaning
In the words

But
She
Could
Feel
The pain
As it burst
In his voice
Like

A wave
Crashing
To the shore

Things life had offered
were nothing
to holding her

in not expecting
to reach the heights
he had
missed the view

He had flown too close
To the waters
Where we cleanse ourselves
Of responsibility
All reason
And was
Drowning
In the scum
That forms there

His soulmates now
were
the onlychildren

of the world
puppies
separated from their mother's teat

                                          too soon

                              forcefully parted
                               thrown into life
                                    separated
                    from blood and companion
                              before they knew
                               how to stand
                                     alone

In the night
he entered
strangers' worlds
walked
corridors
of the museum
of loneliness

galleries
filled
by memory's messages
brought him so close
to her soul
unwelcome wakefulness
that cheated him
of the chance
to return her smile

the biggest part of him
had given him reason
had gone

if he concentrated
he could have
 those times again

Full of questionings
Whatever he had felt
for her
was held tight
inside

Fit to burst
with nowhere to go
his love
was sterile
pointless
it could not be shared
any more
except
to be told
to others

but
where was the point
in that

he could not
keep it in
he could not
let it out

for what reason
would the world
need to see
his misery

that world
was deaf
to his voice
and rightly so

What tormented
his very reason
held no point
or purpose
for them

Did he ever say sorry?

he had said
I want you

he had said
it was wrong
For her to go

he had said
so many things
To say I love you
But
He could not remember
That he had said
Sorry

Ever retreating
From the noise
Of his life

Adulthood
Making the needle stick
And repeat
The words

Working a groove
Until eventually
the matchbox hole
In his soul
Would no longer
Allow it
To play

Searching around
In what might have been

A mechanical repetition
Grinding
In ahead
So that nothing Else could be hurt

A needle
Bouncing
On the turntable
As it turns

On a regular
And monotonous
Revolution
45 times
In a minute

Incomprehensible
Noise

No music
Or refrain
Just the turning

Churning
Rhythm
Of the Lost

Bereft of hope
Bereft of a reason
For the why
Of the past
And the why
of the future

Just guilt
Of a past
Which are given
The chance
He would

                              Most certainly
                                    Repeat
                                     Again

                              A rock'n' roll
                                  Sisyphus

Nothing he could say
Would change
Anything now

There was no one
To hear

 she was gone
but not   gone

                    Nothing he could say
                    Could change anything
                              now

                         understanding
                            That only
                          In unbroken
                         Broken dreams
                          Lay the place
                           They would
                           Ever have
                            To share
                            the words

                          That he always
                          Needed to say

Busted
And so far
From home

If only he had known
Where
That should
be

Lost in a place
So complete
That there was

No return
to passion

for past dreams

Of what might be

What he might
Have become

What a joy
It would have been
To press
Delete
On all those thoughts
All the Falsehoods
And Misunderstandings
Which cluttered
The hard drive
Of his existence

And leave
Just the things
He knew now
To be true

To see her smile
hear her laugh
feel her touch
smell her
taste her

His life appeared

An image
Projected onto
His own space
In time

A
Nevertobeunderstood
Illusion

He comforted himself
that
perhaps
Whatever confusion
And pain
He had endured
From the earliest

Whatever
pain and fear
had Created in him
a Blessing

To chasten
And chase
like light
Bouncing
From
a Swan's neck

                                                        a Peace
                                                         Within
                                                       his pain
                                                          Never
                                                          To be
                                                    Relinquished

A place
To build a dream on

was He in that
Place inside himself

A place where it was safe
To marry
A past Hope
And a future now

To mix them hard
Warm in an elusive sun

With unrelenting love
For the rapidly receding World
Which surrounded
his caged
And hopeless life

When he could love her
He could love the world

His spirit
Wanted to hibernate
To hide
away from his
Dark wet place

To be Lost
In a torpor
Bereft of
Any dream
To spark
Any genuine desire

Seeking
Only
The alcoholic
Comfort
Of gathering to him

Those Worthless comforts
Conceived only to
Consume the world
And starve it of a reason

                              The distillation
                                    Of his life
                                   Lay in the
                                        Night
                                  On the lake
                                        Seen
                          Through the window
                                    Captured
                                 Deliberately
                                 Thoughtfully
                                       By her

                                        Its taste
                                        Enough
                                        To tell
                                        A life
                                    it had had
                                    a purpose

Dancing inside fate
Happy to pay
The Price
It asks
And
Surrender
To what it brings

A love
Which would last
free
From
inconvenient moments
Able to breathe
Uncompromised
By any expectation
Including
Their own
                        No matter
                    How many ways
                        He had tried
                    To dress himself

                To hide And assimilate
                Some form of difference

                He had found himself

Exposed
And naked
In a frozen landscape
Which chilled
His soul

stripped
Every vestige
Of fellow feeling
From his being
Human

He let his spirit
Sneak out
Through
The half opened window
Into the dampness
Of the moon starved night
Water dripped from every rooftop
and gutter
Glistening
Where ever the sparse light touched

Inside the room
his body ached and moaned
Caged
And shackled
By the evidence of
its own slow evolving
Disintegration

His secret place
Required
Passing through
The dapple light
Of woodland
Entering a darking Forest
Climbing a hillside
In a glaring dazzling daylight
Sliding down
Mountainside
releasing
his body
from all control

Then glimpsed
sparkling
Water
A stream
A pool
A sunburned rock
Naked
Like a Sacrifice

In the moments
Unquestioning
Safe
Yielding
To the sometime sweetness
Of being alive

Unexpected
And freely given

                                    Anonymous
                                 In the night
                              His spirit drifted
                         Softly over the earth

                              Making no Mark
                              Where is touched

                               observing only
                                    As birds
                                   Struggled
                             hunkered against
                            the dank darkness
                              unwilling to try
                               to move or fly

The absurd voices
Announced
their intentions

Their road to oblivion
Was reaching
Its inevitable
Denouement

He pondered
Just where
He would most want
to spend
A final hour

Wrapped inside her
Lost in her delight

Sitting in the wild
On a brilliant hillside?

Deep in Woodland
Where a stream runs through?

Always with a dog
Close by

How many times
would he say
I Love you
into an empty night
before he too
was free

They had always promised
Each one to the other
That they would not
Let the other suffer

When the time came
They would do
Whatever was necessary

Time and time again
She had asked
Pleaded with her eyes
And whatever voice
She could find

He had had to deny her
Many More times
Than the thrice
Peter did Christ

He wanted

Needed to be

so far
from that place

the care home
where he had left her

such need
came with
its own particular guilt

that he had abandoned her there

Only those who had
experienced that feeling
could stand
where he stood now

he knew of her willpower

But He did not know how

She had found her way

To the river once again

as she waded
 leadened legged
from skirts weighed down
with stones
 each one so Care fully chosen
 did she
 note the leaves
 signalling an urgent semaphor
by the side of the darkened waters
Did its chill
waken her
to the dancing grasses
the sparkling of the buttercups
amongst the green

Did she see
the soft breeze
charm the light
on the broken surface

into her own ophelia reflection
did she hear
the Sweet exchanges
of the hopeful songsters
before her ears
were dulled
with the deep muffled roaring
of the waters flow

he would wager
it must be so

                    In a sigh
                    too deep
                    for words
                    a final sweet
                        breath
                        leaves
                        her
                        gentle
                        body
                worn out with time

                    a soul
                so necessary
                    to salve
                    the pain
                    in every
                human age

                            Now she was dead
                            The things they did
                            The things they said
                            Had a significance
                            Never understood
                            In their moment

Moments of reality
Long gone
From his life

Lawless
With a freedom
Ready
to spend
to surrender
To trade
For words
Never
To be
heard

He could no longer know
or share
what lay
behind
her eyes

Funeral roses
Cut too late
To die
Too soon

his nostrils
were filled
with
the soft
sweet smell
of
sun scorched earth
after the life giving rains

                    That last night
                    He had dreamed
                        So deep
          They were back in the summer of 69
                  They were beautiful
                        he knew it
                   But he was not sure
                 If she had felt the same

               I love you dropped so easily
                      Amongst them
                    As they wandered
                      In landscapes
                        Familiar
                        And new

                       Cool hippies
                    sitting in the yard
                   smokin' good stuff
                         singing
                      girls dancin'
                    in the moonlight
                      lookin' like

an angel's dream

He had dreamed
that in the night
they had lain together
holding and talking
Fully aware
that everything could be said
and nothing
could be done

now
he could
rest content
in the pleasure
of that moment

so rare
so fleeting

As he walked the places
They had walked together
He began to wonder

Just what her eyes had seen there
What she had remembered

Had it been part of her dying

Goodbye

How sweet
That would
Have been

No hello
No word
Of why
Or how

No forgiveness
Given
In
Perfect
Understanding

TURN AND FACE THE CHANGE

The human condition
Needed re examination
to be Challenged
Confronted
Deconstructed

From the earliest times
He had been taught
To seek companionship

But whenever he found it
Without her
The yearning to be free of it
Swamped his being

He did not feel
Nor want to feel
Part of his kind

He longed
to be separate
And yet....

What he had learned
Was to Trust
at your peril

Or stand
For ever
Always Alone

Surrounded
In a certain
kind
Of light
which admits to
Nothing
amidst
a blackness
Of betrayal

What a narrow
Confined world
He had lived in

Like so many
Things which had shaped
His life
The decision
Was practical
Formed from a pragmatism
Which trapped
The soul

and left it

incarcerated

Denied
Any moment
That would
Fulfil life
And allow
Him to be
Different

swallowed
By the fears
And caged
By the rules of others

Such things
Had Successfully
Destroyed
The wild

Desolating
The world outside
And the life
Within

                                    The closer he looked
                                        All he could see
                                    Was a dissatisfied
                                            Disjointed
                                         disaffection

                                              Denying
                                      Any possibility
                                         Of a natural
                                            Cohesion
                                   Which life had once
                              Evolved through and for

                                   It had been eroded
                                          So quickly
                                       so undintingly
                                            By those
                                       Amongst whom

he had been
So unhappily
Unfortunately
Born

Its only remembrance
In discoloured
grainy
Shadows

Revived
And replayed
As a distraction
To dispel
And The endless
ennui
Of an existence
Free from
Belief
or purpose

He had been
A Moral contortionist
Genuine
Genuflector
driven
By the desire
For anything
that will sparkle

He did not feel
Nor want to feel

Part of his kind

The mass of their ugliness
Was overwhelming the things
He Loved

The delicacy
And strength
Of nature

A nature which
They had stepped outside
Contriving
Absurd
Fantastical
Stories
Of their superiority
And their specialness

A form
confined
Conformed by
the mindless maulings
Of others

Never Reflecting
Nature

always limited
Often starved

Planted in
the barren soil
Of being human

And being human
He had become death

A destroyer
Of this world

They had
time and again
succeeded
in their indifference
To become
The cancerous growth
On the face
Of the earth

an Independent
Thought
never entered
Their birthTodeath
preconditioned
Programming

The sole marker of their sojourn
Written
Scorched
Upon nature's demise

No more

Than automatic

Cogs in the machine

Bulldozing
Beauty
Under
Its inexorable Progress

They had succeeded
In their stupidity
To become
The plague

A cancer
On the face
Of the planet

At a time
that should be mid winter
he glimpsed
full and fair
a woodland path
A spring to summer sky

retelling a dream

when life was shared with her

The sky was hope
the future was now
and stretched forever with her

Hope and fear
vied constantly
For

What he called
Love

Once a word

Now
A whole way
Of being
Tied and tried
By ancient visions

Of what might
Have been
Believe

                              Suddenly
                  years of compromise had gone
            The future which could not hold her
                                     was
                                  at last
                  A place to face the truth

                  No more taking what was there
                            because it was
                        and masking the hurt

                                 of love
                                 A Word
                             Too easily
                            Tripping from
                      A dripping tongue

                            Never known
                          Never properly
                             Understood

                              Until now

And the voice says
We are experiencing
A high volume
Of calls
Please wait
For the next
Consultant
To tell you
What you experience
Is not so

There is
A camaraderie
Amongst
Men
Usually
Of a certain
Age

Men who have not
Can not
Shape the time
In which
They were fired

A separateness
Which allows
Them to recognise
Each other
In the words
They choose
The road to betrayal

                              Searching for others
                                 Who had ridden
                                     On the air
                                   She breathed

                                    He had come
                                     To delight
                        In the 'unseemly' Marks
                                 Of his passage
                                  Through time

                             Marks which would
                                   Offend many
                                  Were precious
                                 To his thinking

                                           Not
                                    To be lost

Or hidden
                           He saw

                        And watched
                        With Sadness

                          Endless

Repetition
Of the arrogance
Fired
egotistical
Cruelty
Which destroyed
The things
He treasured

He had been unable
To redeem
From their
Greedy progress
What he truly had loved

he understood
the Perpetual intractable ugliness
 of his fellows

And realized finally
the importance
Of how
To be
Alone
Separate
Different
Everything he had been told
And taught
Not to be

For He had learned
New love should
be forgot
On two legs
And found
Only On four

every illuminated electric night

when
too many words
had begun
to make
their meaning
confused and unclear

he could not tell
one voice
above another

 he could hear
what were the lies within
but had become unsure

about where
the truth had ever lain

The storm came much later
than promised
but come it did
the rain beat
so strong
so strong

on a half opened window
which would never close

he refused to add another cover
to protect him from
what he needed to feel

letting in the chilled air

                                    pain
                          like fierce rain
                          feeding the sod
                          becoming fresh
                                   again

                              everything
                               had gone
                                 too far

                               there was
                          no turning back

                               no chance
                            to truly live
                                   again

                               he pulled
                           a flimsy cover
                               back over
            then he added another against the chill

in that dread full
interlude
in the night
when the darkness
will not be assuaged
by electric light
an honest hello
had to admit
the smallness of his existence

He compared
the fragile things
which made
his life safe
against those
who lay
on the cold concrete
a short unsafe walk
from where he lay
 in his soft comfort

a walk
he would not dare
or care
to make

                   He was tired
                      of rules
                    it seemed
                  he had passed
                 so many decades
                under the control
                   of others
             always feeling the necessity
                    to obey
              what was best for them
               "for the greater good"
                      or
                 a peaceful life

                   Now he had
                   had enough

what he had sought
and believed in

as the freedom
she had bestowed
he now saw
as simply a void

A place
where he would wander
farther than other times had allowed

where he could project
what grew
so uncomfortably inside
onto that diminished world

There
the emptiness
echoed against itself

Yet still
there were borders

only they were
just more slightly distant
And

freedom just an illusion
conjured in self deceit

When he woke
waiting for dawn
day stretched out
into empty space
that he could never fill

He was looking for a miracle
to see her face
to turn back time
just for an exquisite moment
to find their way back

so many times
visited him
would not leave

not that he wanted them to
even though they usurped
the song of the birds
he so longed to hear

There had been a time
when there had been
nothing that they could not do

he was sure
that it had existed

it was over
no rainbows left
every dream
had died with her

if only she
had been able
to believe in miracles
so could he

A shape
in the darkness

of the night
full of trepidation

Of fear
at the thought
of treading
a foreign landscape

only child
of an only child

In a night
too hot to sleep
planes score the air
seeding poison
to fall
whatever green survives
none untainted

a radio voice
tells what truth
THEY understand

Few are listening
in the diminished
dark

Echoes only
Flickers of light
In shadows
Greyed from the screen

                                        No candle lit
                                        But always burning

What did he think life was for?

To lay waste another's dream?

To draw upon life
From every part
Of the earth

Where it strives
To retain
Its fragile hold

Far too full

Lost in
an automatic universe
Stuffed
with diversion
Requiring
immediate responses
instant answers

No space

To think

To understand

To learn

To create
Or be
Such things
That sit
comfortably
On the earth

Not wanting
More
Than is
Enough

Moment upon
Moment-accelerating-eradication
Isolated from
any True reason
To stay
Or be
Alive

                              In a dream a girl in a red skirt
                                    twirled and whirled
                                          a red scarf
                                          tied tight
                                    around her neck

                                       a black musician
                                      painted his pain
                                            in notes

which cannot be exchanged
for any other goods

not one thing
will be remembered
come their morning light

each one
a thing of the moment
each won
a thing from that night

in the morning

there must remain
some thing
to the rescued

something
for which to care
to draw a smile
and carry each one
through the daylight

until the night
confirmed the sweetest
sweet oblivion
they had sought

where no dreams were allowed

a place to sing

to drown
in silted waters
tracked
by the roots of others
just seeking to survive

before friendly fire
robbed breath away
with its stinging kiss

back to the exotic
riddled rhythm
and
seductive rhyme

beneath a narcotic moon

to danse sweet lies
in unworldly time

courted by the tune
as the red skirt whirled

a red scarf
tied tight
around his neck

Someone
A stranger
sent him
a precious gift
a word
for the aftermath
of the lingering

and precious
warmth
of the sun
But
He had lost it
He had lost the word

He prayed
He would never
lose the feeling

he wanted
to die
in its embrace

In a fire
Brightening circle
The sun
Spread the sea
From Horizon
To shore

a swimmer
Cut The chill of the waters

A crow
applauded
Head bobbing
its delight

desideratum

A place to weave memories
to burn
on the winter night fires

Crackling soundtrack of change
Flashing Sparks and shadows
Blessed transitions
A gift from her grace

Light Yes light
A new special lightness
Smiles then shines
Recording its place
In history
To salve
And replace
A deep missed desire

An absent embrace
So very real
Beautiful
enthralling
Innocent

Light sound
Marking each image
Into its time
Soft
So healing
Innocent
Like it belongs

At times like this
The place one reaches out
For safe softness
Tells
In what arms
Life's dis ease
Can find
A haven

sleep came so easy
Lost in the memory
Of times
that were

That should have been

Other Titles by Geoff Francis

Poetry

SAILORS
ISBN 978-1-907729-25-6

LOST WANDERINGS
ISBN 978-1-907729-17-1

FOUND
ISBN 978-1-907729-23-2

NATURAL HEART
(due 2019)
ISBN 978-1-907729-19-5

Poetry and Photographs

LOVE LOOKS
ISBN 978-1-907729-06-5

I WANT TO SEE
ISBN 978-1-907729-07-2

Fiction

Nature Boy: A Badger's Tale
(due 2019)
ISBN 978-1-907729-18-8

Babylon Farm with Paintings by Geoff Francis

ISBN 978-1-907729-17-1

Or is it? with images by Paul Windridge

ISBN 978-1-907729-20-1

Spirit of the Game

ISBN 978-1-907729-08-9

Spirit of the Game Audio Book

ISBN 978-1-907729-24-9

The Pleasure of Women

ISBN 978-1-907729-12-6

Non-fiction

Stanley Matthews The Black Man with a White Face

ISBN 978-1-907729-02-7

Celebrity Vegetarian Cookbook with Janet Hunt

ISBN 1-85425-017-5

www.bonobo.tv

Samples from other books

FICTION

BABYLON FARM

Extract from Chapter 1

What had been going on? Perhaps it was just as well his memory stretched no further than the present.

'When can we take him away?'

'No more than three or four days, I'd guess. By the way, have you given him a name yet?'

'No, we thought we'd wait and see how he performs. Then we'll choose something to suit his nature. Is that a problem?

'Well, we do like them to have a name before they leave. It makes it easier for the paperwork.'

'I'm sure we can find a way round that. You do know whom my husband works for, don't you?'

'Yes, Mrs Farmer'.

The resentment and disdain in this last reply was scarcely masked, even by the door between him and the speakers.

'Would you like to see him? Perhaps it will help you in deciding on a name.'

A lock was thrown and the door pushed half open on its heavy hinges. A head topped with a white cap appeared first.

'Hold on,' she said over her shoulder. 'I think he's awake. I'll just check. You never know how they're going to react.'

A middle-aged and rounded woman stepped forward. She wore a crisp white overall to just above the knee. The smile on her face was not sincere, yet he felt there was some sympathy in it for him.

Warm and careworn brown eyes met his, as she pressed her face close to check his state of consciousness. He noted the blood vessels burst in what had once been white but now blued into grey, betraying a deep weariness which was about to become annoyance.

'Can I come in now, nurse? I really don't have much time you know... I'm a very busy woman.'

Over the nurse's shoulder he could see a bronzed face framed by a flamboyant, strangely flesh-coloured hat. As the nurse stepped aside he could see that the jacket worn by the woman was in exactly the same shade. He didn't recognise the material, but it was very familiar. It didn't suit her at all. Somehow it clashed violently with her complexion. She was not unattractive in a contrived and superficial sort of way, but there was something about her he could not warm to. Such women aren't sensitive to much but they can sense when they're not appreciated. In a flash his eyes had conveyed a fateful truth. This was a bad start. For all he knew, she could be his wife or lover. Certainly she indicated that she had some sort of control over him. He had shown he didn't like her and she was going to make him pay for that. She turned without a second look.

'We'll pick him up in three days,' she said tersely.

'And the name for the paperwork?'

'We'll call him ... 'she paused, '"Sorrow"!'

His head was buzzing. Sorrow. What sort of name was that? Who had the right to give him such a name? Who had the right to name him at all? How could they do that? He was alone, with time to ponder (there was nothing else to do). But the anger would not subside, frustrated further by the fact that there was no one to ask. Every four hours the nurse arrived. She checked him over. Asking her the questions he held met only with a fake smile.

'You'll have to ask the doctor when you see him,' was the reply to his every enquiry.

'And when will that be?'

With a shrug of the shoulders, she paraded her counterfeit and left.

On the third day the doctor arrived, accompanied by the unsympathetic woman. He was told to get out of the bed and stand straight. His hair, ears, eyes and teeth were given close scrutiny. The nurse then untied the cord behind his back that held the night shirt covering his body. He stood naked and somehow shamed. His modesty was gone. The women looked on impassively. He did not know why he was being treated like this. He didn't even know where he was, and because of this, all he knew was that he needed to comply with their commands. His nakedness seemed to embarrass no one but himself.

OR IS IT

Chapter 1

The Angel that sat on his shoulder was dark. Darker than the night which shared its little light unconditionally with any who sought it.

When the cold entered the autumn air and leaves began to fall, the light which lit his room seemed to gather in all the cold from the world outside and chill the place even more in an extra starkness. The leaves had been dying earlier and earlier year on year.

Sirens chased briefly in a distant street. The car was white and unsafe, its repair unaffordable. On this journey he would not accept death as a companion as he had on every other. On this one it would have to hitch a ride. As he drove, the Angel spoke with words he could decipher, but the voice inside his head delivered them with a strange accent. The voice made pronouncements full of a certainty which was alien to his own opinions and thought processes.

Modern man lost his soul when his ancestors became part of the machine.

Then he was persuaded to feed the machine, not only with his labour but by consuming what it produced. Any resistance he had, had soon became futile.

He remembered someone once saying that all it took for evil to prevail was for the good to do nothing. He had tried to live by such sentiments but had discovered that words were all they were. Everyone he had ever known would avert their eyes at times when it was convenient to them. He had been one of their number for some time now. Yet he still despised them all, and himself, for his weakness.

Chapter 2

What was it like to be alive then? In the Before times that the angel spoke of? Was the truth easier to find, before those around you were hardened by life and hardened to its lies? Now those who ruled were the Survivalists. The ones who believed that survival was the end game and that the end justified any means to attain it. They rode roughshod over any sort of dream except their own material aspirations. Their pragmatic hatred of life wanted only to reduce it to their own subjective misunderstandings of what it should serve.

Theirs was a celebration of the selfish and the self. Under the banner of 'Survival is all that Counts', they had established a thousand mile exclusion zone of fear - with love on the outside. They embraced only the darkest of the dark angels. The angel of fear. In his embrace anything was acceptable. Their only true passion was to steal. Cheating, to haul in the trawler net of greed, was the intention of their every pursuit.

Their dark arts required the betrayal of trust and friendship. Taking, hurting, killing and maiming what had once been good.

Truth had no validity in this world. To a lesser or greater extent, everyone had morphed into each other's fantasies. To attach feelings to a fantasy would only serve to compound the illusion that there is a truth which lies at its core.

He had lived in that world too long. He had believed in truth and this in turn had made him malleable to thefantasies of others who were conscious of their machinations and manipulations. It had cost him dear. Half a million credits extracted by those who had called him friend. Eventually he had learned to say 'No' to the expectations of others, but the damage had already been done long before. Now he had nothing, no one wanted to know him.

But he had what all explorers need - good fortune. However his was not in his luck, which seemed to be bad more often than not. It was in his ability to find something of worth in whatever the journey presented him and to retain the sense of adventure in it. Perhaps it was not so much that his luck was bad, it was simply that he had trusted people. If they told him of a dream they had, he would try with whatever he had available, to help them achieve it. But to lie is easier than working and easier than believing in themselves. Such people he now saw as the devil's spawn. He hoped that some sweet day they would become the victim of love. And would die there. Lost to its cause. Victims of an unrealised enemy, which had lain dormant somewhere inside themselves.

SPIRIT OF THE GAME

Chapter 1

The words of The Who's "Can't Explain" throbbed in his ears. He had played the same song a thousand times.

Today it matched his mind. Never had the words, recorded thirty years before his birth, had such resonance. He was feeling sad. There were some obvious reasons why, but there was also something deep inside which he couldn't touch, or wasn't willing to examine.

He had played the song a thousand times. Today it matched his mind. Never had the words, recorded thirty years before his birth, had such a resonance.

Jamie could still feel the early morning's chill, despite the car windows being locked against it. He would have run the engine but Carol (a true green) had made off with the keys just to make sure he didn't. At least that's how he saw it. He was pissed off with the world, big time. Firstly it was morning, early morning, barely 6 o'clock and that would have been reason enough. Many nights recently, proper rest had been hard to come by. He had been on the internet 'til 2, when he had finally found the right images to help him ease his way into sleep. But good and necessary as it was at the time, that always left him tired and somehow sullied the next morning. And this was that morning.

He looked closely at Carol as she stamped her feet on the pavement to keep warm. She was waiting for the woman who was taking over her alternative health clinic to come and collect the keys. He watched how men who passed looked at her. Even those of his own age. None of the girls on the net looked that good. The cold intensified with his tiredness.

At last the woman showed. Carol handed over the keys. He watched her mouth.

"It's all yours now."

She smiled and held the woman's hands for a few extra moments then released the keys into them before heading towards the relative warmth of the car. Jamie fired up his laptop. Google Earth opened, he clicked on England and eventually Stoke. As he did, the image flashed momentarily of the statue of a footballer. He typed in the postcode of his current location London NW4. Carol climbed into the driver's seat next to him.

Chapter 2

Four weary hours later, they drew up outside a terraced house split to two flats. As the right hand front door opened a dread welled in Jamie's stomach. There stood a tall attractive fit black man, who probably even now could have run him close over 100 metres and Jamie was fast! He had liked Amos. He had been around forever, or at least since a year or so since his dad had left - or rather not come back from a tour. His mum had met Amos at a Womad festival. They had even taken him to a few music events. They were occasional friends, just friends. Then they got married! They had certainly kept that quiet.

He felt betrayed, angry and jealous. They kissed with a passion which was restrained for his sake, but his eyes saw how their hands lingered on each other. His face told them that he had recognised their true longing. He dragged his bags out of the boot and into the hall. Amos pointed the way to his room. Jamie shot there as quickly as possible. He shut the door forcefully, rifled in his bags for the station for his iPod; and as soon as he had set it up, slammed in the player, racking it to maximum volume.

"I'm bleeding for you. You want to cut me into little pieces"

He closed his eyes to beat away the frustration. An innocent throat was cut in the vision of a fleeting memory. There was no solace anywhere. He sensed the intimacy happening in the next room and there was no place for him. He had to get out of there. He slipped out of the room and downstairs to the front door, pausing just briefly to confirm in his own mind that Amos and his mum had no interest in him.

Headphones in his ears and the message of isolation being repeated with each track, he eventually found himself in a park. He sat down on a bench, drew his knees up to his chest staring but not seeing, listening only to his pain. Suddenly a ball intruded on his loneliness. A gang of youths gesticulated at him to kick it back. As he went to control the ball it slipped away. Automatically he stretched out his left foot, rolled the ball onto his instep and began to juggle it before sending it back to the group.

They applauded and catcalled, then beckoned him

over. They were all wearing blue and yellow United shirts with Allen 9 on the back. By the time the kick-about was over the football bond had been sealed. The lads all looked to be about his age; 15 or 16. Peter was a good ball player and probably intelligent in other ways, Jamie thought. On the other hand Joe was not. He was barely past fourteen, thin and wiry. He was afraid of no one and a real head case. A vicious tackler even in the kick around. The others took their lead from Will, the eldest, turned out he was a few days into his eighteenth year. He was an overweight bullyboy who really was no player at all, but a clogger who could be an effective spoiler, he conjectured. And they seemed to think that he, Jamie, was OK.

NATURE BOY: A BADGER'S TALE

Chapter 5

The animal set off into the darkness of the wood. Liam followed. At no time did Liam feel uncertain as to whether he should follow his four-footed guide. Despite the darkness, the further he went, the warmer and safer the forest felt. And the colder and more dangerous the world outside became. Clouds dispersed and uncovered the moon, which shone bright as sunlight revealing a new world. Deepening shadows created strange shapes to right and left. His ears were awakened to new sounds, but he didn't feel discomforted.

The trees became less dense. Another clearing opened before him. At its centre a number of entrances had been excavated. The area was peopled by half a dozen creatures similar to his guide. The smaller ones were romping together in energetic play. They stopped and looked at Liam through their little eyes. Then they recommenced their interrupted games.

The one who had led him there looked back at him. Liam took this as an invitation - an instruction to stay. He dropped his rucksack to the ground, propped his head on it as a pillow and fell into the sweetest sleep to the comforting snuffling sounds of his new companions.

Each day, as he watched the badgers (for this is what the creatures were), he learned from them. He took particular note of the one who had led him there. Over time he gathered that she was something of a fierce 'boss lady'. He gave her the name Boudica after the legendary female leader of the early Britons. He had loved the tales of ancient times and tradition which Angie would sometimes read to him to coax him into sleep.

Intuitively Liam understood the badgers' need to be reclusive, keeping well clear of those of his own kind. In his short life, he had already had enough experience of their cold-hearted fickleness and disloyalty. The search for food forced him to go somewhat dangerously but cautiously close to human habitation. Here the results of the excess and profligacy of people nearly always provided a multitudinous choice of diet. He was amazed and delighted to discover what had been discarded by individuals and shops. The bins at the rear of supermarkets were the richest pickings, and he would always eat royally following a visit there. He made his forays in the darkest part of the night.

THE PLEASURE OF WOMEN

Chapter 1

The railings had been lacquered and painted too many times not to have been amongst those rare survivors of the wartime demand for metal to feed Britain's fighting machine. Perhaps this had been one of the better class areas of Notting Hill Gate in those days and perhaps that alone won their reprieve. If so, it had gone a long way down in a very short space of time. Now the rain trickled laconically down from the pitted ornately pointed tops onto the railings below. He pushed the gate open and began his descent. How quickly the dampness increased. By the time he reached the paint flaked door his nostrils were full of the smell of mildew and decay. It was a smell familiar to anyone who had grown up poor.

For him and his family the post-war changes had efficiently delivered him from that. He had been removed to the suburbs and educated well. Now, with his degree tucked under his arm, he was back amongst the poor, doing his social work bit. And the smell was back in his nostrils. It wasn't ordinary social work though. Not 'straight' social work. The people he worked for were given the cases that the regular authorities (how he and his contemporaries despised that word!) didn't want and wouldn't touch. He knocked on the door.

'Come in,' echoed from deep inside. It was a strong voice, a woman's voice with something of a Scottish accent. He followed it down an unlit corridor, his eyes rapidly seeking to make the necessary adjustments.

'In here,' the voice came again, commanding him to a right turn. He pushed at a half closed door. What greeted him he certainly was not ready for.

There, on a double bed, sat a very large woman, a very large woman indeed! In a shocking day-glo peach nightie! The nylon fabric did very little to constrain her form and its translucence did even less to hide what lay beneath.

He judged that she must be at the very least twenty two stones in weight. He truly did not know where to look and this clearly amused her.

'Sit down,' she ordered him.

He looked around to a black and red plastic armchair, moved the several copies of the Daily Mirror stored there, made himself as comfortable as he could feel and tried to take in the form again. He smiled nervously. He knew it was a nervous smile, but he didn't want it to be.

He had always prided himself on being comfortable with older women. Old men too. He had been brought up to value them and their opinions. Maybe a little too much so. But the sheer presence of this old woman (at least 50 he guessed) was quite awesome in a very uncomfortable way.

'Mrs McCallum,' he started.

'Norma.'

'Norma. I'm Pat.'

He held out his hand nervously. She took it gently and they shook. For some reason he had expected the hand to be hard and clammy as the result of a hard life and a consequence of her physical condition. But it was soft and his hand brought back with it a waft of perfume. Perhaps Rose Water.

'So you are going to look after me,' she said mischievously and smiled again. He looked towards thebedside cabinet. In a glass sat the front row of teeth which he might have expected to make up the major part of the smile. Instead there was a dark and unnervingly ominous orifice.

'Danny asked me to come and see what we can do for you. I understand you have some problems with the social work.....'

'Bastards! Coppers and Social Workers. They're all the same! Bastards!' She began to hit her forehead with the palm of her hand. 'I hate them!' She reached into the glass, fished out the teeth, put them in place and smiled wickedly.

'But I like you.'

He shivered. Perhaps it was the chill in the basement, Or was it that smile?

NON FICTION

STANLEY MATTHEWS:
THE BLACK MAN WITH THE WHITE FACE

INTERVIEW WITH ARCHBISHOP DESMOND TUTU

In the summer of 2008, a special charity match was arranged at the Britannia Stadium, Stoke City's ground, to organise the erection of a statue of Gordon Banks. This was to go in front of the stadium close to where the Three Ages of Stan statues stand.

Amongst the guests for the match were Pelé, the man who said of Stan, "He was the man who taught us how the game should be played" and Archbishop Desmond Tutu who, at that time, had made no public pronouncements about Stan. During the half time interval, Jean was introduced to The Archbishop and handed him a copy of the facsimile of Stan's personal scrapbook. They spoke about Stan's involvement in South Africa and she was pleased to hear the high regard in which the Archbishop held her father. Pelé signed a copy of Stan's autobiography for a later charity auction against his famous quote.

I had been alerted by Jean that the Archbishop would be coming and had tried for a week to organise an interview with him through the Club. However, this had proved unsuccessful, so on the Friday evening I contacted an organisation in the U.S. "We the World" with whom Bonobo TV, our online TV Station, is associated. The Archbishop and world-famous primatologist, Jane Goodall, are their patrons. A direct call to the founder of "We the World" brought an immediate response from the Archbishop's personal assistant and on the Sunday morning we were granted one of two interviews, the other being Sky Sports.

Although we were the first scheduled interview, the Archbishop was running late due to his religious devotions and we stepped aside to take the second slot. I introduced him to the idea of Stan's having been known in Soweto as "The Black Man with the White Face". What he had to say in response to this was nothing that in our wildest dreams we could have expected. So much so that he thought it important to give a full transcript of the filmed interview.

"What I want to say, first of all, is that, you know, we are a sports mad country, both black and white. White South Africans on the whole having been mad on rugby particularly and perhaps cricket and the majority of the black people really love soccer, I mean, you find people who are Manchester fans, I'm Arsenal, actually, (he laughs). Over a very long period of time we were attached to various sporting figures and I clearly remember being mesmerised really by Stanley Matthews's dribbling exploits, he was on the wing most of the time, but he seemed to be able to turn on a we used to say a 'tiki', a small coin that we had, I mean, he was quite amazing, really, how he could confound most defences and so a load of people regarded him, yah, as a hero and it was quite something when he came to South Africa especially going into the townships.

"It wasn't just that this is a sporting great visiting just another country. It had a significance, a white man who had been at the top of his trade coming into the townships at a time when racial discrimination was at its most intense. It was something that had all kinds of ramifications in the fact that it also helped to strengthen our hope for the future. So, it wasn't just, as it were, maybe a sporting gesture or a gesture of magnanimity. It had a very, very profound significance in that it, although you might not have thought that might be the case, it did make a dent in the apartheid armoury because it said there's something quite ridiculous that you should have someone come all the way, ten thousand miles, to do something that was not normal in that country. It just showed how ridiculous our system was as, most of us believed, and one can only pay the highest possible tribute because he needn't have done it, I mean, he went out at the height of his powers having received all kinds of plaudits, the first soccer knight as it were, getting those particular kudos and he could have sat back and put his feet up and nobody would have taken umbridge that he had done so.

"So what he did had an even more enhanced quality about it because he needn't have done it, he wasn't doing it for what it was going to do to his bank account, it was wonderfully altruistic. And so on behalf of our people I want to pay a very, very warm tribute to him and to say that he would not have known just how incredibly significant what he did to our self-esteem, what he did, yah, I mean it made a contribution to people not becoming anti-white because they were able to say there are white people who care about the plight of black people."

POETRY

SAILORS

The boy sat on the quay
With knees
Tucked close
And tight
Safe in his own
Embrace

warmed in the sun
from early morning hours
The stone bench
transferred its gift
Freely
To his body

At a close distance
An old man
Told stories of the sea
of Sailing close To the Wind

Of enchanted shores
Near and far
And
The wonders
Of what lay beneath

Of riches
That should not be traded
which belonged to
the treasure chest
Of the mind

what He re remembered Best
Was when the old man had said
The sea
Is the only place
Now
And for ever
That you can be truly free

Searching there
For her madness
in the space
Between
The waves
And the water
Hopelessness
Would come upon him

LOST WANDERINGS

Love looks like
something
in particular
You would know it
as it
walked
down the street

That was what he was told
And that is what she believed

Underground
her shocking pink pleats
on a two day tan

she would never look lovelier
but how would she find
that one person
who
would confirm
what she knew
in that moment
of her hopefulness

Instead it proceeded
to fumblings in the dark
with a drink to light a hopeful
hopeless spark
As pretty as she'd ever be
but who was there to enlightened her
as she tightened her crutch

Playing deep in her memory
the singer made love
to her gently
from each speaker
of a body broken
phonograph
machine

The Wind crooned
sickly sweet
in a drain pipe
then screamed
freedom
as it found
the cold night air

Snowflakes
played
in candle light
blown
by the outlet from the air conditioning
Someone was inextricably
part of his life
as he sat
beside another.

FOUND

Their words
Sparkling-full-of-laughter
Rained down
In a shower

A shower
after
a long time
travelling

Warm
comforting

Covering
Each part of them

Seeking out
The most intimate

Which
they offered up

Freely

and he felt
the deepest
sagest
love

a love
he welcomed

was happy
to enjoy

a love
they had both
carried
so lightly
for two thirds
of their lives

NATURAL HEART

Love is the thread by which
we hold onto
and are held by life

The quality of that thread determines
whether ours

is an existence of delight
or misery

of indifference or celebration

Like dolphins at play
You are a delight
we are celebration

A tern
Caught within the light
Of the new
moon
Playing sweetly
Gentle on the sea

To be a child
In the church
Of the wild

Swimming there
Rain washing skin
Iridescent blue
Break up on break

Shining sliver sleeper
Slithers
In the mirror of memories

Regrets
sorrow's
sadness and anger
Mingling in the elusive lie

Sweet as chocolate
Bitter as wormwood
To heal the heart
Expel the intangible hurt

Promising hope
To desperate eyes
Gazing full-mooned
Upon an orphaned forever

Laying up
An undesirable store
Against the coldest
Of winters

a dozen crows
on winter wood
stand sentry
over the stillness

hard against
the clear blue
of the day

www.ingramcontent.com/pod-product-compliance
Lightning Source LLC
Chambersburg PA
CBHW032012040426
42448CB00006B/600